DON'T KNOW MUCH ABOUT®

DINOSAURS

KENNETH C. DAVIS
ILLUSTRATED BY PEDRO MARTIN

SCHOLASTIC INC.
New York Toronto London Auckland Sydney
Mexico City New Delhi Hong Kong Buenos Aires

ACKNOWLEDGMENTS

An author's name goes on the cover of a book. But behind that book are a great many people who make it all happen. I would like to thank all of the wonderful people at HarperCollins who helped make this book a reality, including Susan Katz, Kate Morgan Jackson, Barbara Lalicki, Harriett Barton, Rosemary Brosnan, Dana Hayward, Maggie Herold, Jeanne Hogle, and Rachel Orr. I would also like to thank David Black, Joy Tutela, and Alix Reid for their friendship, assistance, and great ideas. My wife, Joann, and my children, Jenny and Colin, are always a source of inspiration, joy, and support. Without them, I could not do my work.

I especially thank April Prince for her devoted efforts and unique contributions. This book would not have been possible without her tireless work, imagination, and creativity.

This is a Don't Know Much About® book. Don't Know Much About®
is the trademark of Kenneth C. Davis.

ISBN 0-439-80615-1

12 11 10 9 8 7 6 5 4 3   7 8 9 10/0

Printed in the U.S.A.   40

First Scholastic printing, October 2005
Design by Charles Yuen

—INTRODUCTION—

Dinosaurs are about the coolest animals that ever lived on our planet. Some of them were huge, some tiny, some odd, and some just plain weird. I think we love dinosaurs because they were big, different, and most of all because they're dead. Dinosaurs fuel our imaginations with wonder!

—Jack Horner, paleontologist, Museum of the Rockies, Montana

How do you make a dinosaur? Yank on its tail. Get it? Dino-sore? Oh, well. Besides a lot of bad jokes, dinosaurs have also inspired some of the most confusing, mixed-up ideas that people have about any creature that ever lived on Earth.

Part of the problem is a long string of "caveman" movies and cartoons like *The Flintstones* that show human beings living with dinosaurs or dinosaurs talking. Some of those movies have also given people strange ideas about when the dinosaurs lived, what they ate, and how they raised their dino babies.

The truth about dinosaurs is really a lot more fascinating and fun than all the silly ideas that some people have about what the dinosaurs were like. During the past twenty years, scientists around the world have made tremendous discoveries that have filled in the gaps in our knowledge of these creatures. For instance, they have found that feathers evolved on dinosaurs before they appeared on birds. They have also learned that many of the things we used to think about dinosaurs were mistakes.

Dinosaurs are one of Earth's great mysteries. By asking and answering questions about dinosaurs, DON'T KNOW MUCH ABOUT® DINOSAURS brings you interesting and intriguing facts about these creatures that roamed the entire Earth for far longer than people have been here. It even tells you how to explore the world of dinosaurs for yourself. When you are done, you will know for sure that being a dinosaur hunter doesn't mean carrying a spear or a club!

WHAT IS A DINOSAUR?

What were dinosaurs like?

Dinosaurs were an amazing group of reptiles that ruled Earth from 230 million years ago to about 65 million years ago. They came in all shapes and sizes, from scurrying creatures the size of chickens to earth-shaking monsters ten times as heavy as modern elephants.

Like today's reptiles, dinosaurs laid eggs and had dry, rough skin. But they were different from present-day reptiles in one important way: They stood with their legs directly underneath them. All other reptiles' legs are bent and sprawled out to the sides of their bodies, making them look like they're always in the middle of a push-up. Most dinosaurs could walk and run easily and well.

Reptiles are animals that usually lay eggs with hard or leathery shells; have dry, scaly skin; and are cold-blooded. (More about being cold-blooded on page 10.) Lizards, crocodiles, snakes, and tortoises are modern reptiles.

Were all dinosaurs big and scary?

It's true that some had serious dino-might! The largest meat eaters could have swallowed you whole. But other meat eaters would just have nipped at your heels, since they were no bigger than chickens. And still other dinosaurs wouldn't have been the least bit interested in having you for lunch. That's because they ate only plants.

Aww, that's cute.

Did dinosaurs swim or fly?

No. But other reptiles of the Dinosaur Age did, and it's easy to get those animals confused with dinosaurs. (See pages 26–27.) Some dinosaurs could paddle across a river if they needed to, but none lived in the water or flew through the air.

Sit, Fifisaurus, sit.

DINOSAUR TIMES

Did early humans keep small dinos as pets?

Only in made-up stories, like the TV show *The Flintstones*! That's because the first humans didn't appear until a whopping 63 million years after the dinosaurs died out.

The earliest dinosaur found so far was named *Eoraptor* (EE-oh-RAP-tur), or "dawn stealer," because it lived at the dawn of the Dinosaur Age. *Eoraptor* was a meat eater that was about as tall as a German shepherd dog. The first *Eoraptor* skeleton was discovered in Argentina in 1991, when a scientist who was about to throw away a rock noticed that the rock had teeth!

Dinosaurs lived during a period of Earth's history we call the *Mesozoic*, or "middle life," Era. (Scientists divide the history of Earth into eras, and the eras into periods.) Dinosaurs lived during all three periods of the Mesozoic Era: the Triassic (try-AS-ik), Jurassic (joo-RAS-ik), and Cretaceous (krih-TAY-shus).

The first dinosaurs, which appeared during the Triassic Period some 230 million years ago, were small and lightweight. Bigger and heavier dinosaurs like *Brachiosaurus* (BRAK-ee-oh-SAWR-us) and *Triceratops* (try-SER-uh-TOPS) appeared in the Jurassic and Cretaceous Periods. Before dinosaurs died out at the end of the Cretaceous Period, some of them had become the largest animals that ever walked the Earth.

TRUE OR FALSE Turtles and crocodiles lived alongside dinosaurs.

True. And believe it or not, they haven't changed much in the past 200 million years. You wouldn't recognize many of the things living in the Mesozoic Era, but some would be familiar—snakes, snails, birds, small mammals, cockroaches, and dragonflies. Sharks, starfish, and clams lived in the water. Trees and plants included evergreens, ferns, and, later, flowering plants.

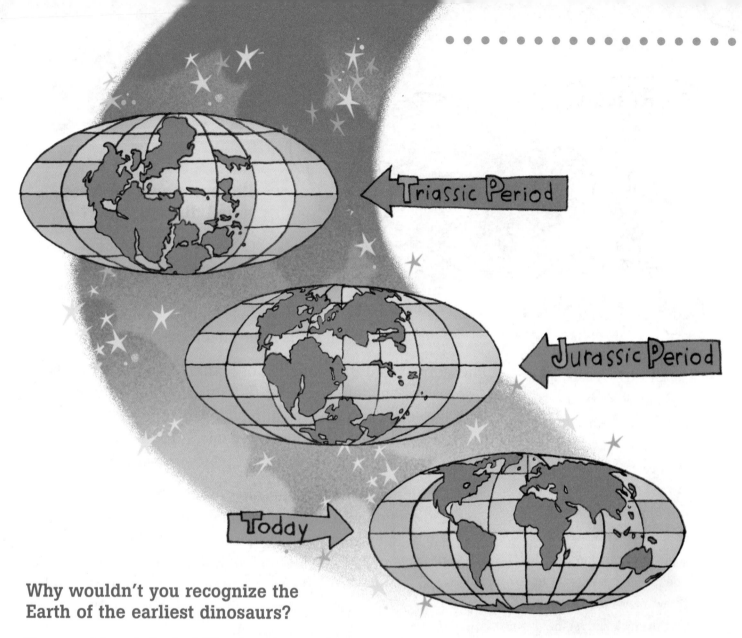

Triassic Period

Jurassic Period

Today

Why wouldn't you recognize the Earth of the earliest dinosaurs?

For one thing, it looked like the picture above! In the Triassic Period, all the land on Earth was one huge continent called Pangaea (pan-GEE-uh). That meant the first dinosaurs could— and did—stroll anywhere they pleased without crossing an ocean. During the Jurassic Period, Pangaea broke into two land masses. And by the Cretaceous Period, today's continents were taking their current shapes.

You also wouldn't recognize the Earth of the dinosaurs because its climates and plants were different from those you're used to. Earth was a warmer place then. The Triassic of the first dinosaurs was hot and dry, with huge deserts spread across the land. In the wetter Jurassic, forests of tall trees started to grow. And during the Cretaceous, winters became cooler and the first flowering plants bloomed.

The reason big pieces of land move over time is because Earth's *crust,* or hard outer shell, is broken into many separate plates. Land sits atop these plates, and the plates move a tiny, tiny bit (about the length of your fingernail) every year. Over millions of years, those tiny movements add up. Today you can still see how the continents once fit together like the pieces of a jigsaw puzzle. In another 150 million years, Earth will look very different again.

Did dinosaurs really "rule the Earth"?

Yes! Not only did dinosaurs spread throughout the world, but they also dominated Earth for an amazing 165 million years. Humans have been around for only 2 million years—the blink of an eye compared to the dinosaurs' reign.

Evolution is the scientific idea that all organisms and living things have developed from earlier forms, as natural selection allowed those with certain traits to survive while others died. The successful traits were passed down from one generation to the next. For example, giraffes with long necks survived because they were the only ones that could reach the nutritious treetop leaves. Giraffes with shorter necks died out because they had to compete with other animals for the lower leaves. Everything that lives on Earth today is thought to have evolved from the planet's first tiny, one-celled creatures.

Were dinosaurs the first living things on Earth?

No, though they were some of the biggest. This time line shows when different life forms appeared on Earth.

4.6 BILLION YEARS AGO	The Earth, moon, and solar system form.
3.8 BILLION YEARS AGO	One-celled life forms develop.
570 MILLION YEARS AGO	Shelled sea animals form.
530 MILLION YEARS AGO	The first fish appear.
400–350 MILLION YEARS AGO	Plants thrive.
350 MILLION YEARS AGO	Amphibians (cold-blooded animals that live in water and on land) appear on land.
330 MILLION YEARS AGO	Primitive reptiles, the first beings to live completely on land, appear. These reptiles would *evolve*, or change, into the first dinosaurs.
230 MILLION YEARS AGO	The first dinosaurs appear.
220 MILLION YEARS AGO	Pangaea breaks up; our current continents first appear.
200–140 MILLION YEARS AGO	The first birds and mammals appear.
125–100 MILLION YEARS AGO	The first flowering plants grow.
110 MILLION YEARS AGO	The present continents form.
65 MILLION YEARS AGO	Dinosaurs mysteriously die out. Some mammals, insects, and others survive.
2 MILLION YEARS AGO	The first humans appear. They make tools, use fire, and eventually learn to communicate.
30,000 YEARS AGO	Modern humans appear.

ON THE MOVE

How many legs did dinosaurs walk on?

a) two   b) three
c) four   d) eight

The answers are *a* and *c*. Dinosaurs came in two- and four-legged models, depending on their lifestyles.

Most meat eaters walked on two feet, with their bodies balanced like seesaws over their hind legs. This made them speedier than they would have been on four feet. It also left their hands free to hold on to their dinners. Most plant eaters walked on four feet because their heavy bodies needed more support. But some plant eaters could balance on their two back feet for short amounts of time. This may have allowed them to make a quick getaway from an attacker or to reach up to higher branches.

Dinosaurs are divided into two groups by the structure of their hip bones. In the hips of *saurischian* (sawr-ISS-kee-un), or lizard-hipped, dinosaurs, one of the bones pointed forward. In the hips of *ornithischian* (or-nuh-THISS-kee-un), or bird-hipped, dinosaurs, all the bones pointed backward.

Why didn't dinosaurs leave tail trails?

I meant to do that.

Because they held their tails straight out behind them for balance when they walked or ran. Most dinosaurs had such heavy heads or such long necks that, without their tails as counterweights, they would have fallen flat on their faces! Tails also came in handy for plant eaters that stood up on their back legs to reach high branches. When they leaned back on their tails, they created a triangular base that kept their bodies steady.

WARM OR COOL?

Are we sure dinosaurs were cold-blooded?

No. Scientists once thought all dinosaurs were cold-blooded, like today's snakes, lizards, and other reptiles. (*Cold-blooded* animals control their body temperatures by taking heat from their surroundings. *Warm-blooded* creatures, such as mammals and birds, make their own heat, keeping their bodies warm no matter what the outside temperature.) Now many scientists think that some dinosaurs were cold-blooded, others warm-blooded, and still others not fully one or the other. It seems that small meat eaters must have been warm-blooded, especially those who caught their dinner at night, when the sun wasn't around to keep them warm. They would have needed the steady energy supplied by a warm-blooded body. Plant eaters, who weren't nearly as active, were probably cold-blooded.

Did dinosaurs like to sunbathe?

A warm-blooded animal needs about ten times more food than a cold-blooded animal of the same size!

We think the cold-blooded ones did. Today's cold-blooded animals warm themselves by sitting in the sun. The blood vessels in their skin absorb the sun's rays to warm their blood, and thereby their bodies. To cool off, the animals stand in the shade or a cool breeze.

Warm-blooded creatures, however, make their own heat by burning up food. They don't need to sunbathe to recharge their batteries.

Which dinosaur had a switchblade?

Like many meat eaters, quick and deadly *Deinonychus* (die-NON-ih-kus) had sharp teeth and strong jaws. But its most deadly weapon was the switchblade-like claw on the second toe of each foot. When attacking, *Deinonychus* probably leaped into the air and kicked its hind legs out in front, slicing open its dinner with one blow. To keep its prized weapons super-sharp, *Deinonychus* held up its claws while running.

Diplodocus's (dih-PLOD-uh-kus) powerful whip-tail was longer than a school bus!

Did all dinosaurs have sharp weapons?

No. Some of the largest plant-eating dinosaurs used their enormous size to protect themselves. *Apatosaurus* (uh-PAT-uh-SAWR-us) might have reared up on its hind legs and come down on top of an attacker. Some of the smaller plant eaters who couldn't do this just tried to look bigger and scarier than they were. The plates on *Stegosaurus* (STEG-uh-SAWR-us) and the huge neck frill (a sheet of bone) on *Triceratops* might have helped with this. The intimidating plates and frills might even have flushed a dark, angry color when their owners were threatened.

Just kidding!

Many plant eaters used their talented tails as whips or clubs. Plated dinosaurs had tails with nasty spikes on the ends. The tails of armored dinosaurs like *Ankylosaurus* (ang-KIH-loh-SAWR-us) ended in heavy, bony clubs.

FAMILIES

Did dinosaurs live in groups?

Many kinds of dinosaurs did. Footprints of the largest plant eaters show that these dinosaurs traveled in groups of a dozen or more. Skeletons of thousands of smaller, duck-billed plant eaters found together tell us that they formed large herds of hundreds or thousands, probably for protection. And small meat eaters, like *Deinonychus*, appear to have hunted in packs so they could attack dinosaurs as much as four times larger than themselves.

Family Reunion, Sommer, Mesozoic Era

Dinosaur trackways (the fossilized remains of a series of footprints) show that in some traveling herds the adults protected the young by walking on the outside of the group.

How were dino babies born?

Most hatched out of eggs, like the majority of today's reptiles. Many dino moms laid their eggs inside huge nests that they dug into the ground. Scientists think many dinosaurs returned to their nests each year.

Did dinosaur mothers sit on their eggs?

Crunch!

Some probably did. For instance, scientists found a skeleton of *Oviraptor* (oh-vih-RAP-tur) in Mongolia sitting on a clutch of eggs. Other dinosaur parents were probably too heavy to rest on their eggs. Instead they kept the eggs warm by covering them with leaves and plants.

The biggest dinosaur eggs were the size of

a) baseballs   b) basketballs

c) Volkswagens   d) eyeballs

This one gets eggcellent mileage.

Explorer Roy Chapman Andrews found the first dinosaur nest known to science in 1923 in the Gobi Desert of Mongolia. Before he found the nest, no one had been sure how dinosaur babies were born.

A *paleontologist* (pay-lee-un-TOL-uh-jist) is a scientist who studies ancient organisms and living things.

The answer is *b*. You might think dinosaur eggs would be enormous, but the largest ever found were only the size of basketballs. The bigger the egg, the thicker the shell. If the eggs had been larger, the babies wouldn't have been able to get out!

Did dinosaurs take care of their babies?

Some did; some didn't. Scientists used to think that dinosaurs laid their eggs and left them to hatch alone, because that's what most reptiles do today. But in 1978, two nests filled with baby dinosaurs and crushed eggshells were found in Montana. The number of babies born at once in the big, bowl-like nests suggested that they had to have a parent's care. The babies' worn-down teeth showed they'd been fed. This was the first sign that dinosaurs looked after their young.

Scientists aren't sure how long dinosaurs lived. Small ones may have lived for only five years or so. But larger ones, especially the long-necked plant eaters, might have lived for one hundred years if they were warm-blooded, and two hundred or more if they were cold-blooded.

DINOSAUR DIETS

How do we know that dinos dined on different dinners?

We have several ways of learning about dinosaur food. Sometimes the stomachs of fossilized dinosaurs hold partly digested, fossilized meals. We can also examine *coprolites,* or the remains of dino droppings. (Sounds like fun, huh?) Some coprolites contain stems, hard seeds, bits of pinecones, and even bones. The most common way to find out what dinosaurs ate is by looking at their teeth and jaws.

Can you guess what kind of food each of the dinosaurs at the top of the next page ate, before reading the descriptions?

The first dinosaurs were *carnivores,* who ate only meat. Later there were *herbivores,* who ate only plants, and *omnivores,* who ate some of each.

Have you tried sprinkling a little lizard on your tree branch? It's yummy.

a) Meat. Powerful jaws and curved, knifelike teeth were good for tearing through flesh.

b) Tough plants. Leaf-shaped teeth that snipped like scissors were best for slicing up plants.

c) Leaves. Peg-like teeth with spaces between them could comb through and pull soft leaves off trees.

d) Plants. Sharp beaks, strong jaws, and flat back-chewing teeth made quick work of vegetation—even pinecones.

Why weren't some dinosaurs told, "Chew with your mouth closed!"?

Not because they didn't have manners, but because they didn't chew at all! Some dinosaurs swallowed their food whole. Meat eaters who did this had throats that could expand to let large pieces of flesh pass through. Plant eaters who didn't chew had a different approach—they let their guts do the work. (Find out how on page 17.)

Why did some plant eaters eat all day?

Because large plant eaters had small mouths and enormous stomachs to fill. It took a lot of plants to fuel the big animals, since most plants don't deliver many *calories*, or units of energy. Some scientists think that the biggest plant eaters had to eat as much as a ton of food—amounting to a bus-sized pile of vegetation—every day!

With all that eating, dinosaur teeth wore down pretty quickly. But not to worry—another tooth just grew up in place of a worn-out one and pushed the old one out. Plant eaters like *Edmontosaurus* (ed-MON-toh-SAWR-us) had nearly one thousand teeth at a time. That must have kept the prehistoric tooth fairy busy!

PLANT EATERS

cycads   evergreen   fern   horsetail   hungry

Why didn't dinosaurs eat grass?

Because there wasn't any around yet! Instead the ground in the Mesozoic Era was covered with ferns and other low, bushy vegetation. Plant-eating dinosaurs snacked on these plants and also on evergreen and fir trees, pinecones, fruit, seeds, and, later, flowers. Magnolias, which were one of the first flowering plants on Earth, are still around today. They look almost the same as they did in the Cretaceous Period. Other plants from the Age of Dinosaurs you might recognize include cycads, evergreen trees, ferns, and horsetails.

Did different plant eaters fight over the tastiest leaves?

They might have. Each dinosaur's diet depended on which plants it could reach and what its mouth, teeth, and jaws could process. (Check out the teeth on page 15.) Since different dinosaurs ate different plants, several kinds of herbivores could graze together, each munching at a different height. To find enough to eat during cold or dry spells, many plant eaters might have *migrated,* or moved from one place to another at the same time each year, to find lusher areas in which to feed.

How did some plant eaters "chew" with their guts?

The peg-like teeth of giant plant eaters like *Diplodocus* weren't much good for crushing and grinding food. So the "chewing" was done in the gizzard, with the help of *gastroliths,* or stones these dinosaurs swallowed along with their food. The stones churned around in the gut to grind up the vegetation. (Chickens swallow grit or sand for the same reason.) Meat eaters didn't need to make this stone soup because meat is easier to digest than plants.

 Strong muscles pushed food down *Brachiosaurus's* long neck into its gut, in much the same way you squeeze the last of the toothpaste out of the tube.

Fresh cracked rubble with your salad, sir?

Please!

One of the largest dinosaurs ever to walk the Earth was the 140-foot-long *Seismosaurus* (SIZE-moh-SAWR-us). Discovered in New Mexico in 1979 by paleontologist David Gillette, *Seismosaurus* was so big it took scientists eight years to dig it up. In the dinosaur's stomach area, Gillette found more than 240 smooth gastroliths. Most were peach sized, but one was as large as a grapefruit!

MEAT EATERS

What were meat eaters' best weapons?

a) claws
b) teeth
c) brains
d) eyes
e) speed
f) all of
   the above

He may have claws, teeth and speed, but you have SPUNK!

The answer is *f*. Meat-eating dinosaurs used more than their sharp claws and gigantic teeth to catch their dinners. They also used their heads. These hunters had bigger brains than plant eaters because they needed keen senses, fast reflexes, and the ability to plan an attack.

Many meat eaters also had large eyes and may have had sharp color vision. (Plant eaters likely had poorer, black-and-white vision.) And though some meat eaters were faster than others, they all had compact, muscular bodies that moved on two strong back legs.

A *predator* is an animal that hunts other animals for food. The animals a predator kills and eats are its *prey*.

Was *Tyrannosaurus rex* really the king of dinosaurs?

In many ways, yes. *Tyrannosaurus rex* (tih-RAN-uh-SAWR-us REKS), often called *T. rex,* was as big and heavy as a bus—and much more ferocious. *T. rex* might have eaten its weight, six to seven tons, in meat each week. That's as much as ten or twelve cows! Though there were a few meat eaters who were bigger, *T. rex* was probably the most deadly because of its robust, sturdy build. No wonder this giant predator's name means "tyrant lizard king."

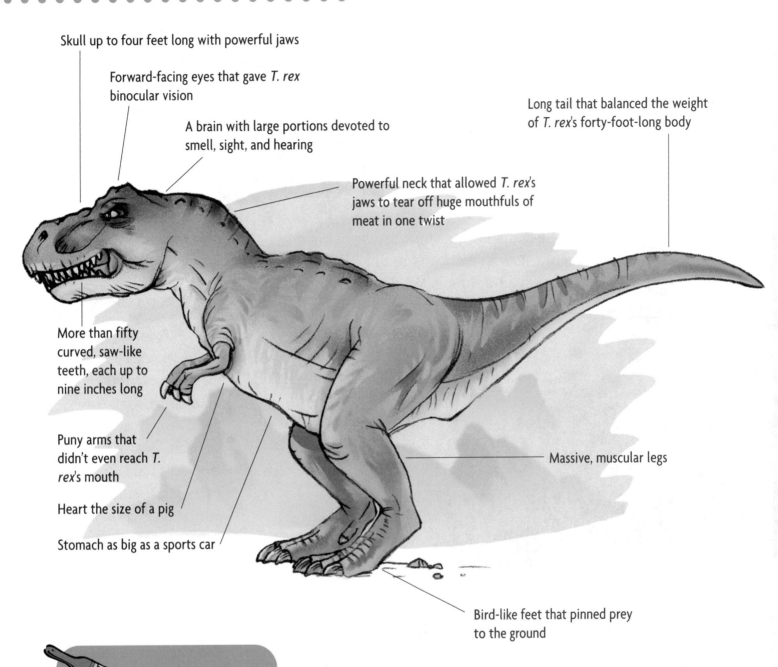

Skull up to four feet long with powerful jaws

Forward-facing eyes that gave *T. rex* binocular vision

A brain with large portions devoted to smell, sight, and hearing

Long tail that balanced the weight of *T. rex*'s forty-foot-long body

Powerful neck that allowed *T. rex*'s jaws to tear off huge mouthfuls of meat in one twist

More than fifty curved, saw-like teeth, each up to nine inches long

Puny arms that didn't even reach *T. rex*'s mouth

Heart the size of a pig

Stomach as big as a sports car

Massive, muscular legs

Bird-like feet that pinned prey to the ground

The meat eater *Troodon* (TROH-oh-don) had especially large eye sockets. Scientists think *Troodon* might have had such good sight (for a dinosaur) that it could see in the dark, catching prey others might miss.

TRUE OR FALSE **Meat eaters ate only other dinosaurs.**

False. Meat eaters, especially smaller ones, ate just about anything that moved. On the menu were smaller lizards, insects, birds, and little, rat-like mammals. (And not just the flesh of these critters—the bones, brains, guts, and all!) Scientists also think at least one Captain Hook–like dinosaur, *Baryonyx* (BARE-ee-ON-iks), speared fish with its huge, curved claws. Some carnivores even appear to have eaten members of their own family! Still other meat eaters didn't kill their own food at all, but ate the leftovers of other carnivores. These animals were called *scavengers*.

How did *T. rex* launch an attack?

Some scientists have suggested that *T. rex*, because of its short arms and possibly slow speed, was mainly a scavenger of dead animals. While it's likely that *T. rex* scavenged when it could (why not take advantage of a free meal?), most scientists agree that *T. rex* was primarily a hunter. When attacking, *T. rex* might have hidden and surprised its prey instead of trying to beat it with speed.

Which *T. rex* has been nicknamed the "Colossal Fossil"?

She's a *T. rex* named Sue. The skeleton was named after Susan Hendrickson, the amateur fossil hunter who found her in 1990. Sue is the largest, most complete, and best preserved *T. rex* skeleton ever found. Because she's so complete, Sue can teach us a lot. The South Dakota farmer on whose land she was discovered sold her to the Field Museum in Chicago for $8.36 million. There she's on display, and scientists can study her beautiful bones.

Mom! Billy's trying to eat me again!

For a long time scientists thought the dinosaur *Oviraptor*, whose name means "egg thief," liked to have eggs for breakfast. That's because they found fossilized *Oviraptor* skeletons near nests of what looked like *Protoceratops* eggs. But it turned out that the nests were really *Oviraptor* nests. The dinosaurs were protecting them. Poor *Oviraptor* was named for a crime it didn't commit!

Which dinosaurs really knew how to use their heads?

The *pachycephalosaurs* (pak-ih-SEF-uh-loh-SAWRS), or thickheaded dinosaurs. Pachycephalosaurs' skulls had super-thick domes, some of which were nine solid inches deep! These domes were built-in crash helmets that were used to head-butt attackers. Male pachycephalosaurs probably also head-butted one another to compete for mates or to become the leader of their herd. Mountain goats do that today.

Scientists once thought *Parasaurolophus* (PAR-uh-saw-ROL-oh-fus) used its long crest like a snorkel to breathe underwater. But there weren't any holes at the top of the crest to let in the air, so that can't be true!

Which dinosaurs were the best musicians?

The title goes to the *hadrosaurs* (HAD-roh-SAWRS), or duck-billed dinosaurs. Though these dinosaurs were named for their broad, toothless bills, they're also well known for their bony head crests.

Scientists think some duck-billed dinosaurs used their crests like musical instruments. When they blew air through the hollow tunnels in their crests, the vibrating air would make a loud sound, the way it does in a trombone or foghorn. The sound each dinosaur made depended on the size and shape of its head crest. Some hadrosaurs, like *Edmontosaurus* (ed-MON-toh-SAWR-us), might have made themselves heard by inflating a balloon of skin over their noses the way bullfrogs inflate their throats today. Since hadrosaurs lived in large herds, they may have used these noisy noses to warn each other of danger or to find mates.

ARMORED, HORNED, AND PLATED DINOSAURS

Stegosaurus is famous for having the smallest brain for its body size of any known dinosaur. Though its body was as long as a van, its brain was the size of a walnut! The brain was so small that scientists once believed *Stegosaurus* had a second brain in its tail to control the rear part of its body. Today we know that's not true.

Q: What do you call a sleeping *Stegosaurus*?

A: A *Stego-snorus*!

What kind of dinosaurs had bones on the inside and the outside?

The *ankylosaurs,* or armored dinosaurs, were one group. These stocky reptiles were built like armored tanks. They were covered from head to tail with bony spikes, plates, and knobs. The only places usually left unprotected were their soft stomachs. *Euoplocephalus* (YOO-oh-ploh-SEF-uh-lus) even had shutters on its eyelids! If their armor alone didn't discourage a predator, the tough creatures could defend themselves with the clubs at the ends of their muscular tails.

Which dinosaurs wore collars, but not neckties?

The *ceratopsians* (SER-uh-TOP-see-ans), or horned dinosaurs. These plant eaters had large, bony, collar-like frills around their heads. Some were so big they made up half the dinosaur's skull! Especially large frills may have looked threatening, warning predators away like a sign that said DON'T COME ANY CLOSER! Scientists think frills also attracted mates and helped dinosaurs recognize one another. Frills couldn't have done much to protect a dinosaur's neck and shoulders, because some of the bony sheets were as thin as eggshells.

How many horns did Triceratops have?

Here's a hint: A *tricycle* has three wheels. *Triceratops* had three magnificent horns. Aside from the short horn atop its nose, *Triceratops* had two brow horns, each more than three feet long. Scientists think these two sharp horns were used more for head-wrestling another *Triceratops* over mates than for attacking predators. But *Triceratops* could run quickly over short distances to charge an attacker if it needed to. Strong and stocky like a rhinoceros, the dinosaur was built to withstand the impact of such a charge.

Including its frill, *Triceratops*'s six-foot-long skull was more than ten times bigger than your own! Even though the frill had large holes, the skull weighed as much as an ox.

LONG-NECKED DINOSAURS

Why did the huge long-necked dinosaurs have such small heads?

The head of *sauropods* (SAWR-uh-PODS), or long-necked dinosaurs, had to be small and light because they were so far away from their bodies. (The farther away something is from the center of your body, the harder it is to hold up. Try holding a bag of apples close to your chest. Then hold that same bag out at arm's length. What happens?) Sauropods' extra-long necks were also light, because they were made of semi-hollow bones.

Overall, the sauropods were the longest, heaviest, and tallest animals that have ever lived on land. Thick, pillar-like legs held up their barrel-like bodies. Their strong, whip-like tails balanced out their long necks.

Hi.

Did *Diplodocus* do handstands?

The answer is, almost certainly, no. But one set of trackways does seem to show *Diplodocus* walking on its front legs only. Scientists think the animal might have been floating in water, pushing itself along with its front feet. At one time, scientists thought the enormous sauropods lived in water to support their great weight. Now we know they lived on land but could swim if they had to. (Or else *Diplodocus* really was doing a handstand!)

Why were the sauropods *Apatosaurus* and *Brontosaurus* so similar?

Because they were the same dinosaur! Scientists found two similar skeletons in Colorado and Wyoming in the 1870s. They named the first one *Apatosaurus* and the second *Brontosaurus* (BRON-toh-SAWR-us). Later it turned out that the two skeletons were really the same species. Until 1975 many museums and books used the name *Brontosaurus.* However, scientists now use the name *Apatosaurus* for the dinosaur, since the skeleton given this name was found first.

AIR AND SEA LOOK-ALIKES

Sea reptiles included ichthyosaurs (IK-thee-uh-SAWRS) and mosasaurs. With big eyes and long beaks, ichthyosaurs looked like modern dolphins. They were speedy swimmers powered by strong tails. Mosasaurs were giant swimming lizards with flipper-like limbs and powerful tails.

Why didn't dinosaurs ever fly overhead?

Could they have been afraid of heights? No, actually, these land animals couldn't fly. But prehistoric reptiles called pterosaurs (TER-uh-SAWRS) did sail through the air above the dinosaurs. Dinosaur look-alikes also lived in the prehistoric oceans—reptiles called plesiosaurs (PLEE-see-uh-SAWRS) and mosasaurs (MOSE-uh-SAWRS). Many of these marine and air reptiles looked a lot like dinosaurs, so it's easy to get them confused.

What happened to pterosaurs' arms?

They *evolved* into wings! Pterosaur "arms" had four fingers, three of which were short and had little claws on them. The fourth finger was enormously long and supported a layer of skin that was the wing. Some pterosaurs probably flapped their featherless wings like birds do. Others spread them out and soared like gliders. No one knows how these winged reptiles moved around on the ground.

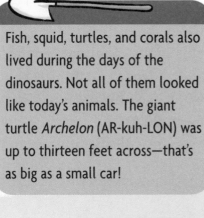

Some people joke that the plesiosaur *Elasmosaurus* (eh-LAZ-muh-SAWR-us) may be the model for Nessie, the fabled monster said to live in Scotland's Loch (Lake) Ness. *Elasmosaurus* could raise its head high above the water's surface to search for fishy prey. Like other plesiosaurs, *Elasmosaurus* had a sturdy body and long, narrow flippers that it used to paddle through the water.

Fish, squid, turtles, and corals also lived during the days of the dinosaurs. Not all of them looked like today's animals. The giant turtle *Archelon* (AR-kuh-LON) was up to thirteen feet across—that's as big as a small car!

Did pterosaurs have tails?

The first pterosaurs, called *rhamphorhynchoids* (RAM-foh-rink-oyds), had short legs, long tails, and ranged in size from that of modern sparrows to that of swans. Later pterosaurs, called *pterodactyls* (TER-oh-DAK-tils), were larger and short-tailed. They looked like enormous bats. Among the pterodactyls was the largest flying animal ever, *Quetzalcoatlus* (ket-SAL-koh-AT-lus). This creature's body was the size of a human's, but its thirty-six-foot wingspan was bigger than that of some small airplanes!

Another well-known pterodactyl was *Pteranodon* (ter-AN-uh-DON), whose head measured about six feet long from its crest to its skinny beak.

RECORD SETTERS

Who weighs in as the dinosaur heavyweight champ?

Argentinosaurus (ar-jen-TEEN-oh-SAWR-us), a South American giant who was discovered in Argentina in 1987. From the few bones that have been removed from the ground so far, scientists think *Argentinosaurus* might have weighed as much as one hundred tons. (To compare, today's heaviest land animal, the African elephant, weighs up to seven tons.) That makes *Argentinosaurus* not only the number-one dinosaur heavyweight, but the heaviest land animal ever to walk Earth!

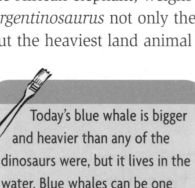

I'm not fat. I'm just big-boned.

Today's blue whale is bigger and heavier than any of the dinosaurs were, but it lives in the water. Blue whales can be one hundred feet long and weigh up to 150 tons.

How long was the longest dinosaur?

Nearly half a city block long! This giant plant eater, who currently goes by the nickname "Rio Negro Giant," was about 160 feet long and weighed at least eighty tons. The dinosaur was found in Argentina in 2000 and hasn't even been named yet because scientists are still digging up and studying its bones.

Whew.

Which dinosaur had the best view?

Sauroposeidon (SAWR-oh-poh-SYE-don), a relative of *Brachiosaurus,* appears to be the tallest dinosaur found so far. This "Lizard Earthquake God"—so named because it probably shook the ground when it walked—took in the view from eyes sixty feet above the ground. You would have had to stretch way up just to reach its knee! *Sauroposeidon* also had the longest neck of any known animal—forty feet from head to shoulders. Single *Sauroposeidon* neck bones are up to four feet long.

I love a parade!

A Giant False Alarm: In the 1970s, paleontologist "Dinosaur Jim" Jensen found bones belonging to two enormous dinosaurs in Utah. Because the bones were so huge, he named the dinosaurs *Supersaurus* (SOO-per-SAWR-us) and *Ultrasaurus* (UL-truh-SAWR-us). At first it seemed that *Ultrasaurus* would take the crown as the heaviest dino. But now it appears that *Ultrasaurus* was really a combination of *Supersaurus* and *Brachiosaurus* bones.

The smallest dinosaur weighed about as much as a

a) bulldozer

b) newborn human baby

c) German Shepherd dog

The average dinosaur was about the size of a modern sheep.

The answer is *b.* The smallest dinosaur known so far is *Compsognathus* (komp-SOG-nah-thus), which weighed only about seven pounds. *Compsognathus* was three feet long and not much taller than a chicken. Though it didn't fly, its bones were light and hollow like a bird's. *Compsognathus* sped around on skinny legs, gobbling up lizards, frogs, snails, and insects with its small, sharp teeth.

In 2000 Chinese scientists uncovered an even smaller meat eater, *Microraptor* (MY-kroh-RAP-tur). But no one is sure whether the fifteen-inch dinosaur skeleton they found belonged to an adult or a youngster.

If the fastest human raced the fastest dinosaur, who would win?

The dinosaur. We can't be absolutely sure which was the fastest dinosaur, since we can only judge dinosaurs' speeds by how they're built and how far apart their footprints are. But it appears that *Struthiomimus* (STROOTH-ee-oh-MY-mus), or "ostrich-mimic," could probably reach speeds of about forty miles per hour. (The fastest humans run at about twenty miles per hour.) *Struthiomimus* needed to be fast because it had no armor, horns, or teeth with which to defend itself.

WHAT HAPPENED TO THE DINOSAURS?

Where are the dinosaurs today?

Dinosaurs, as we think of them, are *extinct,* meaning their species no longer exist. After flourishing for 165 million years, dinosaurs mysteriously died out about 65 million years ago. We don't know if it happened gradually over millions of years, or more quickly over a few thousand years, or all at once in just a year or two. No one knows for sure what happened.

But we do have some guesses. Most scientists think that a huge space object (an asteroid or comet) smashed into Earth at the end of the Cretaceous Period. The impact of the crash would have set half the planet on fire, causing poisonous acid rain. Ash and dust from the collision might have blocked the sun for months, maybe even years. In the darkness, plants would not have been able to grow, and many animals lucky enough to survive the blast, fires, and acid rain would have starved.

Wow, pretty... What is it?

Are any dinosaurs around today?

To find some, just look overhead. Believe it or not, birds are considered to be dinosaurs. Though there has been a lot of disagreement over this idea, most scientists now think that birds evolved from small, lizard-hipped, meat-eating dinosaurs who lived in the early Jurassic Period. Fossils show important links between *Compsognathus*, the small carnivorous dinosaur that ran on long, skinny legs; *Archaeopteryx* (AR-kee-OP-tuh-riks), the earliest known bird; and living birds today. (*Archaeopteryx* is not a direct ancestor of modern birds, though.) *Archaeopteryx* had dinosaur's teeth, jaw, claws, and long, bony tail, but a bird's wings and feathers. Other bird-like dinosaurs had feathers or feather-like fuzz.

Less closely related to dinosaurs are today's alligators and crocodiles. These reptiles have skulls like those of dinosaurs, and they and dinosaurs are descended from the same ancestors (the *archosaurs*, or "ancient lizards").

Some people have come up with especially strange reasons why the dinosaurs died out. They have suggested that dinosaurs died from boredom, committed suicide, were hunted by hungry aliens, or even were "drowned" in their own droppings!

Did everything on Earth die out with the dinosaurs?

More than half the species that were living at the end of the Cretaceous died out with the dinosaurs, but the rest survived. Flying reptiles died out, but birds, insects, crocodiles, snakes, and lizards survived. So did many frogs and small mammals that could bury themselves in the ground. In the seas, fish survived, but all the marine reptiles except the turtles died out. The dinosaurs died out in the most mysterious and dramatic disappearance of a group of animals in the history of Earth.

What signs do we have that there was a Cretaceous asteroid crash?

We don't have the asteroid itself—it would have exploded when it hit Earth. But we do have a 186-mile-wide *crater,* or bowl-shaped depression, along the Mexican coast. The crater, named Chicxulub (shik-soo-LOOB), lies partly under the ocean and partly under the land, and was made 65 million years ago.

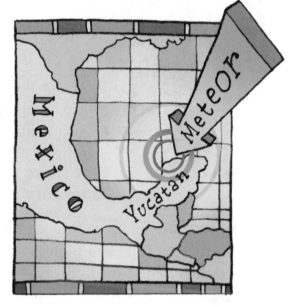

Layers of rock 65 million years old also hold clues. The impact of an asteroid large enough to create Chicxulub would have covered Earth with a layer of clay rich in a metal called iridium. Iridium is rare in most Earth rocks—but not in asteroids. Scientists have found a layer of iridium in 65-million-year-old rock. They have also found a layer of soot, which would have come from the widespread fires.

Could Earth really be hit by a space rock?

Yes. Most asteroids and comets never come near Earth as they travel through space. But some can, and we know that some actually have. There are about 100 huge craters around the world that scientists think were created by space rocks smashing into our planet. One you can see—and walk down into—is Barringer Meteor Crater in northern Arizona. The crater is 50,000 years old and nearly two and a half miles wide!

What are some other guesses about what might have happened 65 million years ago?

More than one hundred ideas have been presented about why the dinosaurs died out. Whole books have been written trying to answer this difficult question! But few of these theories explain why some died and others survived. Some suggest the dinosaurs died because

- they were poisoned by new kinds of plants
- several huge volcanic eruptions spread gases and dust that cooled the atmosphere
  - a huge number of caterpillars ate all the plants, leaving the dinosaurs to starve
  - they caught a disease that spread to other dinos
  - the number of small mammals increased, and those mammals ate so many dinosaur eggs that few dino babies hatched.

Was there anything good about the dinosaurs' death?

Yes. For one thing, we'll never have to come face-to-face with a living *T. rex*! But even more important is the fact that, if the dinosaurs hadn't died out, we might not be here. The small mammals that survived the dinosaur extinction evolved into new species to replace the dinosaurs. Eventually those small mammals evolved into us!

HOW DO WE KNOW WHAT WE KNOW?

This was no "boating accident".

How do we know about the dinosaurs and their times?

From fossils, mainly. Fossils are the remains of organisms and living things that have been preserved in rock. The dinosaur remains we dig out of the ground are dinosaur bones and fossils of bones. Fossils can be as obvious as an entire dinosaur skeleton or as subtle as an imprint of a leaf.

How are fossils made?

Conditions have to be just right for fossilization to occur. Dinosaur bones that became fossils were usually buried quickly, most likely in or near a river or lake. There, as the dinosaur's flesh was eaten or rotted away, the bones sank into the soft ground and were covered with sand and mud. This stopped them from rotting or being washed away. Over millions of years, more layers of mud and sand covered the bones until they were deeply buried. Minerals seeped into the skeleton, altering the bones and turning them to fossils. (Yes, the bones sometimes actually turn to stone!) The surrounding mud and sand also often turned to rock under pressure from all the layers above.

Many fossils aren't full skeletons because bones often scatter before fossilization begins.

Did all dinosaurs become fossils?

No. In fact, not many did at all. Many dinosaurs' bones were too small and breakable to become fossils. Also, many dinosaurs died in dry areas, where their bodies were eaten or rotted away forever. Scientists say that about ninety-five out of every hundred species that have ever existed on Earth are now extinct. Since only a very few creatures left fossils, we'll never know about them.

Are bones the only thing that can fossilize?

No. It's true that, in most cases, only the hard parts of a dinosaur were preserved. But sometimes dry sand or volcanic ash covered an animal and mummified the whole body. This left a fossil impression of the dinosaur's skin or of its soft insides. Still other times, dinosaur footprints, droppings, or nests—but not the dinosaurs themselves—were preserved. These impressions are called *trace fossils.*

These fossils, along with the rock and any plant or animal fossils that are near them, are the only information we have about dinosaurs and the way they lived. Scientists must work like detectives, piecing together as much of the fossil puzzle as they can to create a picture of a world none of us has ever seen.

Here's what different kinds of dinosaur fossils can tell us:

Teeth—what and how a dinosaur ate

Skin—the texture of the skin

Organs—the size, placement, and structure of internal organs like the heart and brain

Bones—the fact that dinosaurs recovered from broken bones and lived with diseases like arthritis. Bones also give us clues about the size and placement of dinosaurs' muscles, because we can see where the muscles attached.

Nests and eggs—how dinosaurs had babies, how the babies grew inside their eggs and continued to grow after they hatched, and that some dinosaur herds acted like families

Coprolites (dung)—what dinosaurs ate

Trackways (footprints)—that many dinosaurs traveled in groups; how many feet they used and how fast they traveled. Footprints that are close together show that a dinosaur was walking; those that are farther apart show it was running. You can see this for yourself by walking and running on wet sand!

The thinking parts of dinosaurs' brains were smaller than those of most mammals. That means dinosaurs probably couldn't have learned new things as easily as a monkey or a dog can.

What's the answer to number four?

Does brain size tell us how smart dinosaurs were?

Not really. Brain size alone isn't as important as how complex a brain is and how big it is compared to the size of the body. We know that meat eaters had bigger brains in relation to their bodies than plant eaters did. No dinosaur had a very big brain, but on the whole they must have been big enough. If they hadn't been, dinosaurs wouldn't have survived so long.

Could dinosaurs taste, hear, and feel?

It's hard to tell, but we do have some clues. Many dinosaurs had tongues, and they could probably taste their food like today's animals can. We know that dinosaurs could hear. The *T. rex* named Sue had an ear bone that transmitted sound, and hadrosaurs (and probably others) likely made noise. And as for dinos' sense of touch, that's hard to say. Anything they touched would have had to make an impression through tough, scaly skin!

How can scientists tell how old a fossil is?

By studying the rock and soil that surrounds it. One way to do this is by measuring the rock's level of uranium. Uranium is an element that slowly changes to lead over time. The more lead is present in a rock, the older the rock is.

FINDING THE FIRST FOSSILS

When were the first dinosaur fossils found?

No one will ever know. But the first recorded find—dinosaur teeth in China—dates back 3,500 years. No one knew about dinosaurs at that time, so the people who found the teeth decided they belonged to a dragon! Chinese records note that "dragon bones" were also found about 1,700 years ago. Since dragons were thought to bring good fortune, fossil bones were ground up and used to make medicines and special magical powders. Even today, some traditional Chinese medicines use tiny amounts of these "dragon powders."

Who first realized that dinosaur fossils came from ancient reptiles?

In 1824 British scientist William Buckland described a fossil jawbone with large teeth that had been found near Oxford, England. Buckland said the fossil came from a meat-eating lizard he named *Megalosaurus* (MEG-a-lo-SAWR-us), or "giant lizard."

The following year a British doctor and fossil collector named Gideon Mantell became the first to identify dinosaur fossils as a completely new kind of animal. (Many versions of the story say the fossils were actually found by his wife, Mary Ann, while she was accompanying him on a house call. But no one knows for sure.) After

One tribe of Native Americans, the Piegan people of Alberta, Canada, thought dinosaur skeletons belonged to "the fathers of buffaloes." Englishmen three hundred years ago believed a dinosaur thigh bone came from an elephant or even a giant human being. No one could imagine that any reptile could grow that big or look so different from modern lizards.

finding the strange teeth and bones in southeast England, Dr. Mantell guessed that they belonged to a giant reptile, probably a giant iguana. He named the creature *Iguanodon* (ih-GWAHN-oh-don), or "iguana tooth."

I'm not so "terrible" once you get to know me.

Other people found fossils in England and elsewhere, but it wasn't until 1842 that a British scientist named Richard Owen realized all the fossils had some things in common. Owen said the bones must belong to a group of animals that lived long ago, a group entirely unknown to science. He named them *Dinosauria,* or "terrible lizards." (In Greek, *deinos* means "terrible" and *sauros* means "lizard.") Though today we know that not all dinos were terrible, the name stuck. Dino-mania had begun.

Where do dinosaurs get their names?

From the first person to describe their fossils. The discoverer might choose a name that describes the dinosaur, such as "terrible claw": *Deinonychus.* Or the name might tell where the fossil was found—can you guess in which U.S. state *Utahraptor* (YOO-tah-RAP-tur) was first discovered? Other names honor a person. *Herrerasaurus* (huh-RARE-uh-SAWR-us)

As more dinosaur bones were found, a sculptor created a display of giant dinosaur models around London's Crystal Palace in 1854. Before he finished the *Iguanodon* model, the sculptor held a dinner party for twenty-one guests inside it!

We'd like a table near the fourth and fifth metacarpal, please.

was named after Victorino Herrera, the Argentinian goat farmer who first noticed the fossil sticking up out of the ground.

How did dinosaurs cause a war—65 million years after their death?

They inspired "Bone Wars" between two famous fossil hunters, Edward Drinker Cope and Othniel Charles Marsh, in the 1870s and 1880s. Both men were searching for dinosaurs in Wyoming and Colorado, where lots of fossils were being discovered. In their attempts to be the first to uncover new dinosaur remains, Cope and Marsh spied on each other's digs and paid "fossil rustlers" to steal the other's finds. Many people were shocked at their behavior, but the rivalry did lead to the discovery of 136 dinosaur species, including *Apatosaurus, Stegosaurus, Triceratops, Diplodocus,* and *Allosaurus* (AL-oh-SAWR-us). In fact, the two dug up so many bones that even today, more than one hundred years later, scientists haven't finished sorting through them all!

A CHRONOLOGY OF DINO FIRSTS

1824 William Buckland describes *Megalosaurus* fossil.

1825 Gideon Mantell describes *Iguanodon* fossil.

1842 Richard Owen coins the word *Dinosauria*.

1858 American paleontologist Joseph Leidy describes the first reasonably complete dinosaur skeleton, near Haddonfield, New Jersey.

1868 English scientist Thomas Huxley first proposes that dinosaurs and birds are related.

1902 Barnum Brown discovers the first fossils of *Tyrannosaurus rex,* at Hell Creek, Montana.

1908 George and Levi Sternberg find the first impression of dinosaur skin, belonging to an *Edmontosaurus,* in Wyoming.

1923 Roy Chapman Andrews and his crew discover the first dinosaur nest known to science in the Gobi Desert of Mongolia.

1972 Jim Jensen finds huge fossils he names *Supersaurus* at Dry Mesa Quarry in western Colorado; in 1979 he finds bones there of an even larger animal that he names *Ultrasaurus.*

1978 Jack Horner finds *Maiasaura* "nursery," the first dinosaur eggs and nests in North America, at Egg Mountain, Montana.

1987 *Argentinosaurus,* the heaviest known dinosaur, is discovered in Patagonia, Argentina.

1990 Sue, the most complete *Tyrannosaurus rex* skeleton ever found, is uncovered in South Dakota.

1991 *Eoraptor,* the earliest known dinosaur, is found in the Valley of the Moon, Argentina.

1993 *Giganotosaurus,* one of the biggest meat eaters, is discovered in Argentina.

1996 *Sinosauropteryx* (SIGH-noh-sawr-OP-ter-iks), the first dinosaur found with primitive feathers, is discovered in China.

1999 *Sauroposeidon,* the tallest known dinosaur, is found in Oklahoma.

2001 Scientists in Gansu province, China, find a trackway containing 100 dinosaur footprints, including an enormous print four feet long and three feet wide.

2001 In China, paleontologists discover the fossil of a nonflying dinosaur that had feathers attached to its body.

2002 Researchers create a computer model to calculate how fast *Tyrannosaurus rex* could run, and determine that *T. rex* may not have been able to run at all because it was so big.

2003 Fossils of a distant *T. rex* relative found in Madagascar provide the strongest evidence to date that some meat-eating dinosaurs were cannibals—that they ate, among other things, their own kind.

Who finds dinosaur fossils?

Anyone can. You just have to look in the right place!

As you might guess, paleontologists discover most fossils. They look for dinosaur fossils based on what they know about when and where dinosaurs lived. Sometimes they're lucky and locate dinosaur bones sticking up out of the ground, or out of a hill or cliff. This happens most often in deserts or canyons, where soil and rock have been worn away by wind and rain.

But not all dinosaur bones are found by paleontologists. Farmers, miners, and other people who have reason to dig in the ground have discovered bones by accident. Maybe you'll find a dinosaur fossil someday!

How are dinosaur bones taken out of the ground?

Verrrry carefully! It often takes months, or even years, to *excavate*—uncover and dig up—a whole skeleton. The picture below shows what often goes on at a dig site.

Scientists map and photograph the site before any fossils are removed. Every bone is numbered and recorded as it is found.

A tent shelters fossils and workers.

Tools include hammers, chisels, picks, and paintbrushes.

Big tools—drills, jackhammers, or explosives—remove large areas of hard rock.

Gloves, goggles, and hard hats protect workers.

Workers brush fossils clean and coat them with hardener for strengthening.

Scientists cover fossils with a layer of tinfoil or wet tissue paper, then add a protective layer of plaster of paris. The foil or tissue paper makes the plaster easier to remove later on.

When the plaster of paris has hardened, workers cut away the rock beneath the bone and add more plaster to form a full "jacket" around the fossil.

Workers take the protected fossil to a museum.

What happens to the fossils at the museum?

After they carefully remove the plaster and tissue, technicians use tiny tools to chip away at the rock that remains around the fossils. Sometimes they place the fossils in acid baths that dissolve the stone without hurting the fossil. To remove the last stubborn bits of stone, technicians often use air-powered tools or even dental drills while looking at the fossil under a microscope. The job can take weeks or months.

Once all the bones are cleaned, workers may make an exact copy of each one. This is done by making a rubber mold of the bone and then pouring a mixture such as fiberglass and liquid plastic into the mold. The mixture hardens with time. Museums often put these lightweight casts on display instead of the real fossils, which are delicate and very heavy.

Do the fossilized bones snap together like Legos?

Unfortunately for museum workers, no. The bones of living dinosaurs were held together by muscles and tendons. With these long gone, the bones must often be wired together, one by one, and mounted on a metal or plastic frame.

Putting a dinosaur skeleton together is like assembling a complicated jigsaw puzzle. This is where the maps and photographs taken at the dig site come in handy! Still, pieces of the skeleton are often mixed up, missing, or broken. For clues to how the bones fit together, and to reconstruct any that are missing, paleontologists often study the bones of other dinosaurs or of living animals.

Where in the United States can you see dinosaur fossils outdoors?

Nearly every state has at least one dinosaur fossil site. Some states have working quarries where you can watch paleontologists in action or even help out! Some of the top dino sites in the United States include:

- **Dinosaur National Monument** in Colorado and Utah, where you can see a rock wall studded with hundreds of huge dinosaur bones.

- **Dinosaur Valley Museum**, also in Colorado, where you can watch paleontologists prepare fossils. The museum also has "day digs" and weeklong programs where you can help dig up fossils.

- **Dinosaur State Park** in Connecticut, where you can make a cast of a dinosaur footprint to take home. You have to bring your own supplies, but park rangers will show you how to make the cast.

- **The Museum of the Rockies** in Bozeman, Montana, where you can tour a re-creation of a *Maiasaura* nesting ground.

- **Dinosaur Valley State Park** in Texas, where you can see some of the best-preserved sauropod, hadrosaur, and theropod tracks in the world.

Where can you see great fossils indoors?

- The National Museum of Natural History, Smithsonian Institution, Washington, DC

- American Museum of Natural History, New York City, NY

- Field Museum, Chicago, IL

- Peabody Museum of Natural History, New Haven, CT

- Academy of Natural Sciences, Philadelphia, PA

- The Science Museum of Minnesota, St. Paul, MN

- Museum of Life and Science, Durham, NC

- Carnegie Museum of Natural History, Pittsburgh, PA

- Lawrence Hall of Science, University of California, Berkeley, CA

RE-CREATING DINOSAURS

Do paleontologists ever make mistakes?

Yes. Gideon Mantell put *Iguanodon*'s thumb claw on top of its nose. It stayed that way until more complete *Iguanodon* skeletons were found more than forty years later. Edward Cope was horrified when his rival Othniel Marsh told him in 1870 that Cope had reconstructed *Elasmosaurus* with its head on the end of its tail! And until recently, *Apatosaurus* appeared in museums with the head of *Camarasaurus* (KAM-uh-ruh-SAWR-us).

These mistakes happen because fossils are often incomplete, mixed up, and confusing. We're always learning new things as scientists find more fossils and do more research. So stay tuned for new developments!

Scientists have named about one thousand different *species*, or kinds, of dinosaurs, and about twenty new species are found every year.

Will dinosaurs ever come back to life?

Though it's fun to imagine *Jurassic Park* jumping off the screen, it's pretty safe to say that you'll never come face-to-face with a living *T. rex*. To re-create long-extinct dinosaurs, we'd need dinosaur DNA, the code that exists in nearly every one of the body's cells. We'll probably never have dinosaur DNA in good enough condition to use to bring a dinosaur to life. But dinosaurs are "alive" in other ways: in museums; in books, movies, and TV; and in the dinosaur relatives who live today.